DEDICATION:

For my wonderful Tūtī Lilia Wahinemaika'i Hale who told me these riddles on a worn green picnic table on the Waimānalo Coast and finished by saying, "Share."

Aloha au iā 'oe.
- Kimo Armitage

Bishop Museum Native Hawaiian Culture and Arts Program

This project is funded under the Native Hawaiian Culture and Arts Program. The views and conclusions contained in this document are those of the authors and should not be interpreted as representing the opinions or policies of the U.S. Government. Mention of trade names or commercial products does not constitute their endorsement by the U.S. Government.

Kamahoi Press is a division of Bishop Museum Press.

Bishop Museum Press
1525 Bernice Street
Honolulu, Hawai'i 96817
www.bishopmuseum.org/press

Printed in Korea

Design by Angela Wu-Ki

ISBN 1-58178-035-4

He Mau Nane Hawai'i
HAWAIIAN RIDDLES

Na Kimo Armitage i haku

Na Meleanna Aluli Meyer i kaha ki'i

KAMAHOI
PRESS

Uliuli me he mau ʻuala, keʻokeʻoke me he hau lā,
ʻula me he ahi, ʻeleʻele me he lānahu lā.

As green as potatoes, as white as snow, as red as fire,
as black as coal.

2

Pane (Answer): *Ka ipu.* (A watermelon.)

3

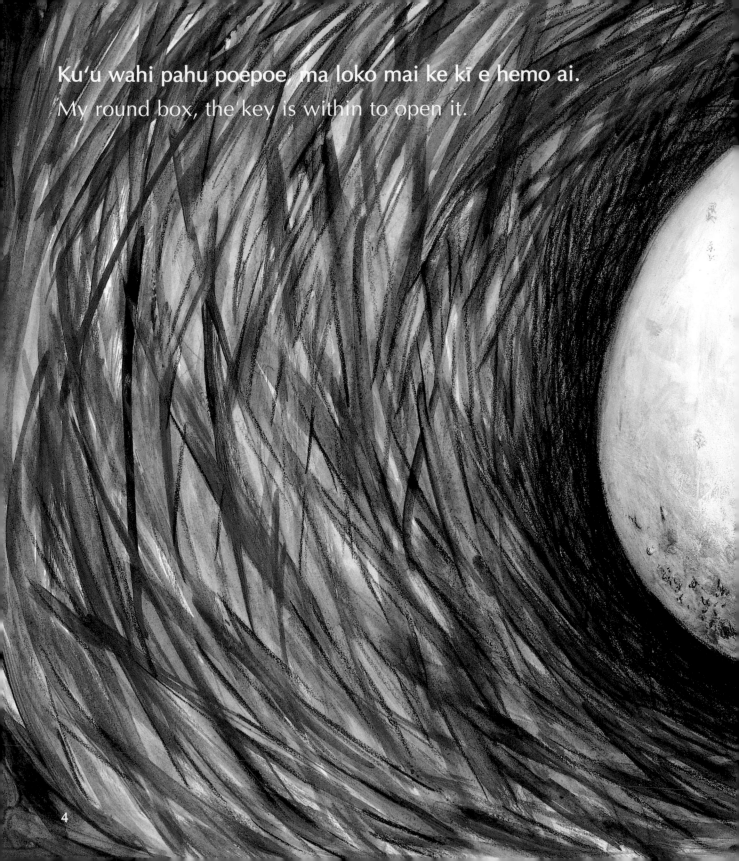

Ku'u wahi pahu poepoe, ma loko mai ke kī e hemo ai.
My round box, the key is within to open it.

Pane (Answer): ***Ka hua manu.*** *(The bird's egg.)*

'Ekahi kapa, 'elua kapa, loa'a aku ka 'i'o ma loko.

One covering, two covering, then you come to the meat inside.

Pane (Answer): *Ka hua kukui.* (The kukui nut.)

Ku'u ana 'ula, kū lālani nā koa kapa ke'oke'o.

My red cave where the soldiers stand in rows dressed in white.

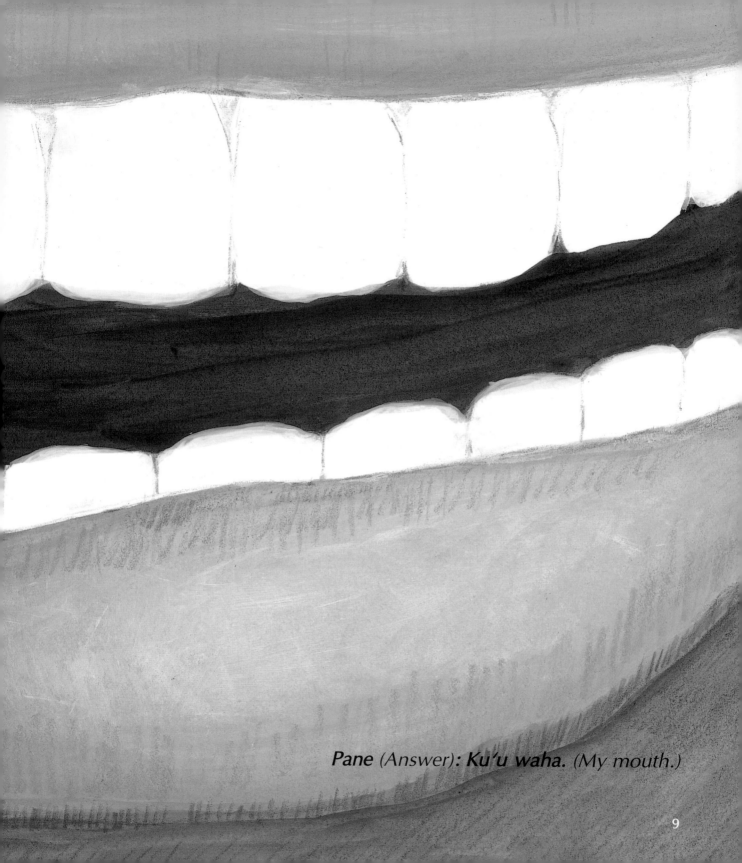

Pane (Answer): **Ku'u waha.** (My mouth.)

Ku'u wahi hale, 'ewalu o'a a me ho'okahi pou.
My house with eight rafters and one post.

Pane (Answer): Ka māmalu. (The umbrella.)

11

Ka iʻa nona ka honua.
The fish that owns the earth.

12

Pane (Answer): **Ka honu.** (The turtle.)

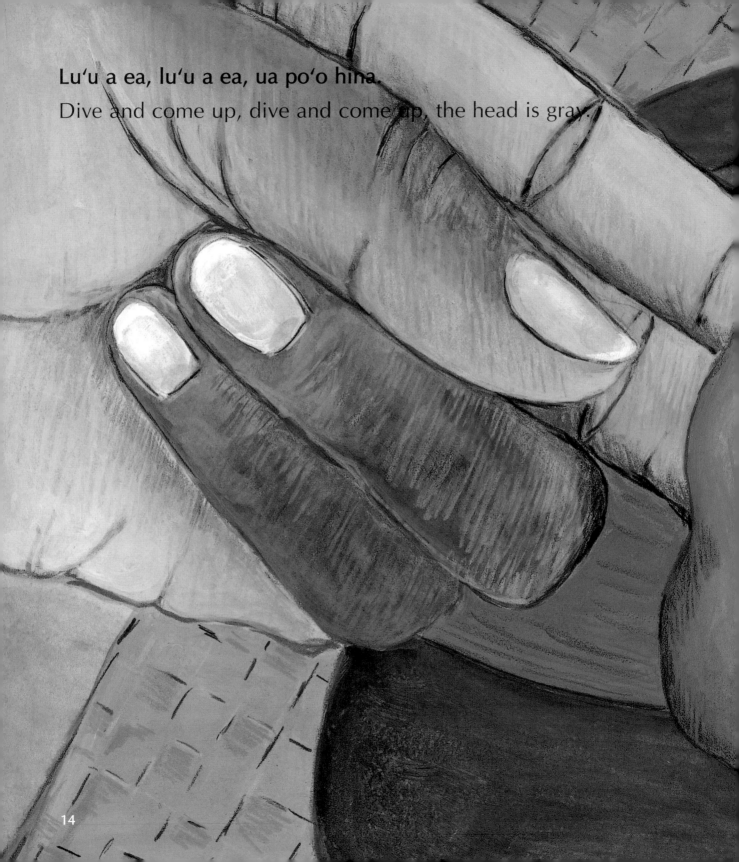

Lu'u a ea, lu'u a ea, ua po'o hina.
Dive and come up, dive and come up, the head is gray.

14

Pane (Answer): **He miki 'ai.** (A finger of poi.)

Ku'u wahi holoholona, 'ewalu ona lima.
My little animal with eight hands.

16

Pane: (Answer): Ka he'e. (The octopus.)

17

Hānau mai, ua poʻo hina.
When it is born it has gray hair.

18

Pane (Answer): **Ka pua kō.**
(The flower of the sugar cane.)

Lahilahi ke kua, a lahilahi ke alo, i kapa nā iwi, i waho ka naʻau.

The back is thin, the front is thin, the bones are on the sides, and the innards are on the outside.

Pane (Answer): ***Ka lupe.*** (The kite.)

Ku'u pūnāwai kau i ka pali.

My spring up on a cliff.

22

Pane (Answer): *He hua niu.* (A coconut.)

Ku'u wahi i'a, 'a'ohe unahi.
My little fish without scales.

24

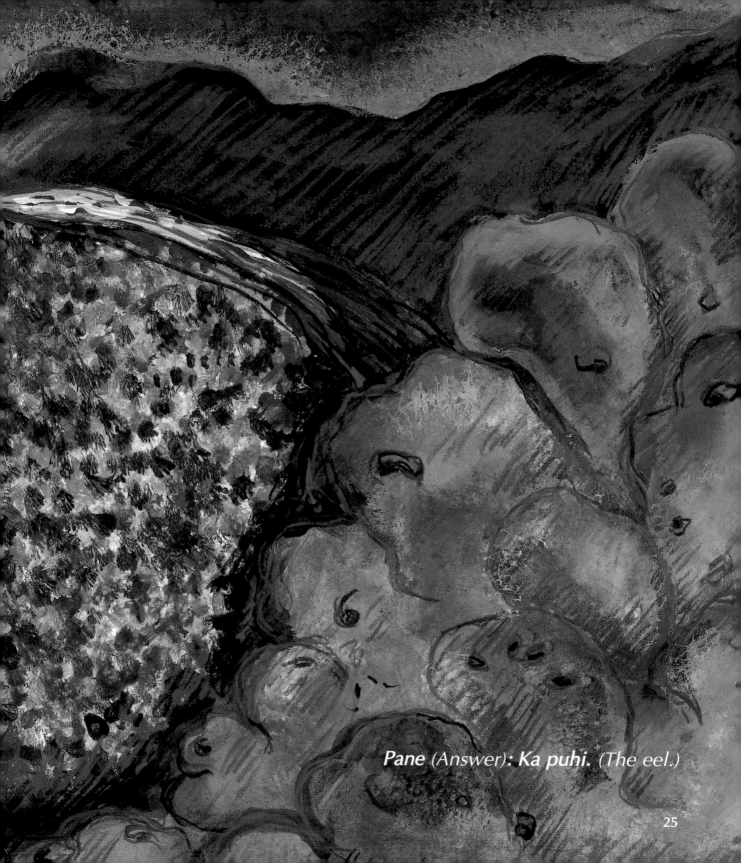

Pane (Answer): *Ka puhi.* (The eel.)

A lau a lau ka 'ālinalina, ho'okahi 'ōpihi kō'ele.
Many small shellfish, one large shellfish.

Pane (Answer): Ka mahina a me nā hōkū.
(The moon and the stars.)

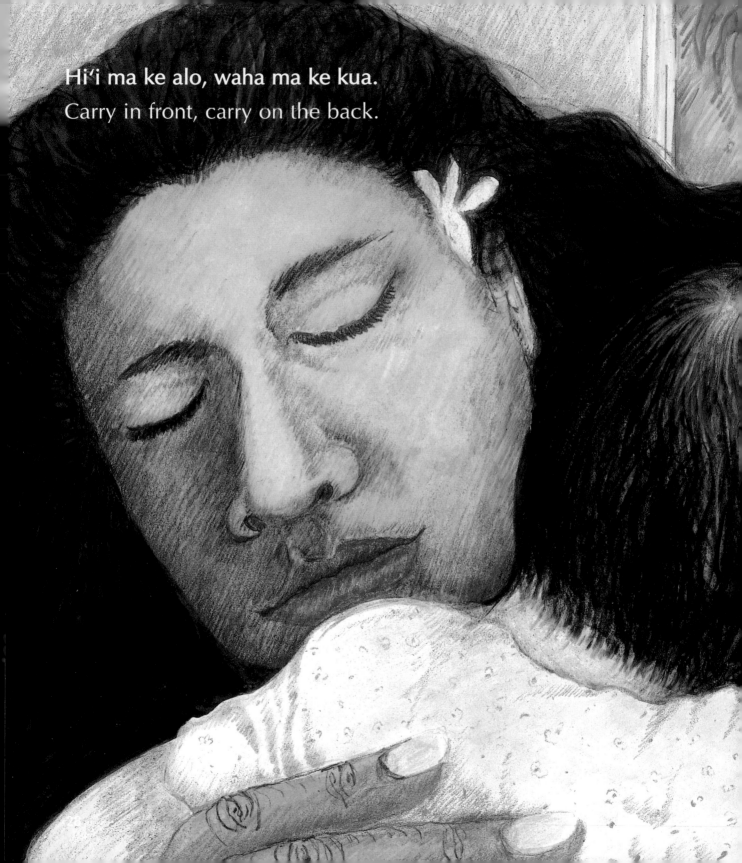

Hiʻi ma ke alo, waha ma ke kua.
Carry in front, carry on the back.

Pane (Answer): **Ke keiki.** *(A child.)*

29

GLOSSARY

ANIMALS

he'e – octopus

honu – turtle

i'a – fish

manu – bird

puhi – eel

COLORS

'ele'ele – black

hina – gray

ke'oke'o – white

'ula – red

uliuli – green

BODY

iwi – bone

kua – back

lima – hand

niho – teeth

po'o – head

FOOD

hua – egg

ipu – watermelon

kō – sugar cane

niu – coconut

'uala – sweet potato

NATURE

ahi – fire

ana – cave

hōkū – stars

honua – earth

mahina – moon

pali – cliff

pua – flower

pūnāwai – spring